"Death never comes at the right time, despite what mortals believe. Death always comes like a thief." — Christopher Pike, *The Last Vampire*

How to use this planner:

Death or being incapacitated can be a drain on your family, both emotionally and financially. Hence this use of this planner is quite a serious business. A well informed plan can make a huge difference in what is left for your loved ones.

Use this planner to update all the relevant information about your contacts, legal and health issues, financial and business affairs and many more. This practical information contained in this planner can play an extremely important role and can help your near and dear ones to sort out vital information at the time of need and can be a very valuable gift to them.

Fill all the relevant information in the planner and keep the same in a secure location. Also please keep updating the information as and when needed and whenever the details keeps changing. Sufficient extra pages have been provided for the same

However please note that this planner is neither a legal document nor a substitute for a Will. It is advisable to consult a lawyer regarding Estate planning

CONTENTS

QUICK GUIDE TO LOCATIONS 6-7

PERSONAL & FAMILY
MY PERSONAL INFORMATION 8-9

MY MARITAL HISTORY 10-12

MY SPOUSE 13-21

MY FAMILY HISTORY 22-26

MY MEDICAL INFORMATION 27-35

EMERGENCY NOTIFICATION 36-37

BUSINESS & LEGAL
MY LEGAL DOCUMENTS 38-47

MY INSURANCE POLICIES 48-54

MY EMPLOYMENT 55-59

MY FINANCIAL INFORMATION 60-68

MY REAL ESTATE 69-70

MY UTILITIES 71-73

MY VEHICLES 74-76

MISCELLANEOUS INFORMATION
MY PETS 77-79

MY MEMBERSHIPS & CHARITIES 80-81

FINAL WISHES
FUNERAL ARRANGEMENTS 82-86

NOTIFICATION IN CASE OF DEATH 87-90

ADDITIONAL NOTES 91-94

DATE UPDATED: _____

QUICK GUIDE TO LOCATION OF MY IMPORTANT DOCUMENTS

Document / item	LOCATION
Address book - personal	
Address book - professional	
Adoption or legal guardianship papers	
Bank account information – check books, statements, debit cards, ATM cards, etc.	
Birth Certificate	
Credit cards – cards, statements, etc.	
Debts owed to me	
Deed	
Disability records & insurance	
Disposition of remains – prepaid burial plots, donor arrangements, etc.	
Divorce papers	
Employment – earnings & leave statements, contracts, etc.	
Family tree & other information	
Household effects inventory	
Income tax records	
Information on my inheritances	
Insurance policy – health	
Insurance policy – life	
Insurance policy – long term care	
Insurance policy – professional	
Insurance policy – property (mortgage, homeowners, etc.)	
Insurance policy – vehicle	
Investment records – stocks, bonds, 401K, IRA, etc.	

QUICK GUIDE TO LOCATION OF MY IMPORTANT DOCUMENTS

Document / item	LOCATION
Key – safety deposit box	
Keys – home	
Keys – other properties	
Keys – vehicles	
Keys or combination - P.O. Box	
Lease	
Marriage certificate	
Military service records	
Miscellaneous debts I owe	
Naturalization papers	
Passport	
Pet records – vaccination, medical, AKC registration, etc.	
Power of attorney	
Social Security card	
Vaccination records	
Vehicle records – loan, title, registration, etc.	
Will, living will, etc.	

DATE UPDATED: _____

MY PERSONAL INFORMATION

FULL NAME: _____

MAIDEN NAME: _____

SOCIAL SECURITY NUMBER: _____

DATE OF BIRTH: _____

PLACE OF BIRTH (include name of hospital, city, county, state, country): _____

_____

_____

CURRENT HOME ADDRESS: _____

_____

_____

LOCATION OF HOUSE KEYS: _____

_____

CURRENT MAILING ADDRESS: _____

_____

_____

LOCATION OF POST OFFICE BOX KEYS OR COMBINATION: _____

_____

_____

DATE UPDATED: _____

CURRENT STATE OF LEGAL RESIDENCE (state in which I vote): _____

DRIVER'S LICENSE STATE & NUMBER: _____

HOME TELEPHONE: _____

CELLULAR TELEPHONE: _____

HOME FAX NUMBER: _____

PERSONAL E-MAIL ADDRESS(ES): _____

PERSONAL WEBSITE ADDRESS: _____

MARITAL STATUS: _____

TOTAL NUMBER OF BIOLOGICAL, ADOPTED, & STEPCHILDREN: _____

LOCATION OF MY PERSONAL ADDRESS BOOK: _____

LOCATION OF MY PROFESSIONAL ADDRESS BOOK: _____

LOCATION OF INFORMATION REGARDING FAMILY TREE & HISTORY: _____

DATE UPDATED: _____

MY MARITAL HISTORY

MY CURRENT MARRIAGE:

NAME OF SPOUSE: _____

DATE & PLACE OF MARRIAGE: _____

LOCATION OF MARRIAGE CERTIFICATE: _____

_____

_____

SPOUSE'S SOCIAL SECURITY NUMBER: _____

SPOUSE'S DATE OF BIRTH: _____

SPOUSE'S PLACE OF BIRTH: _____

SPOUSE'S HOME ADDRESS: _____

_____

_____

SPOUSE'S HOME TELEPHONE: _____

SPOUSE'S E-MAIL ADDRESS: _____

_____

SPOUSE'S PERSONAL WEBSITE ADDRESS: _____

_____

SPOUSE'S EMPLOYER: _____

ADDRESS OF SPOUSE'S EMPLOYER: _____

_____

_____

SPOUSE'S WORK TELEPHONE: _____

DATE UPDATED: _____

SPOUSE'S E-MAIL ADDRESS: _____

NAME & TELEPHONE OF SPOUSE'S SUPERVISOR: _____

_____

_____

MY PREVIOUS MARRIAGES:

NAME OF FORMER SPOUSE: _____

DATE & PLACE OF MARRIAGE: _____

_____

DATE & PLACE OF DIVORCE: _____

_____

LOCATION OF DIVORCE PAPERS: _____

_____

_____

FORMER SPOUSE'S CURRENT HOME ADDRESS: _____

_____

_____

FORMER SPOUSE'S CURRENT HOME TELEPHONE: _____

_____

FORMER SPOUSE'S CURRENT WORK TELEPHONE: _____

_____

FORMER SPOUSE'S CURRENT E-MAIL ADDRESS: _____

_____

DATE UPDATED: _____

NAME OF FORMER SPOUSE: _____

DATE & PLACE OF MARRIAGE: _____
_____

DATE & PLACE OF DIVORCE: _____
_____

LOCATION OF DIVORCE PAPERS: _____
_____
_____

FORMER SPOUSE'S CURRENT HOME ADDRESS: _____
_____
_____

FORMER SPOUSE'S CURRENT HOME TELEPHONE: _____
_____

FORMER SPOUSE'S CURRENT WORK TELEPHONE: _____
_____

FORMER SPOUSE'S CURRENT E-MAIL ADDRESS: _____
_____

DATE UPDATED: _____

MY SPOUSE

NAME OF SPOUSE: _____

DATE & PLACE OF MARRIAGE: _____

_____

LOCATION OF MARRIAGE CERTIFICATE: _____

_____

_____

SPOUSE'S SOCIAL SECURITY NUMBER: _____

SPOUSE'S DATE OF BIRTH: _____

SPOUSE'S PLACE OF BIRTH: _____

SPOUSE'S HOME ADDRESS: _____

_____

_____

SPOUSE'S HOME TELEPHONE: _____

SPOUSE'S E-MAIL ADDRESS: _____

_____

SPOUSE'S PERSONAL WEBSITE ADDRESS: _____

_____

SPOUSE'S EMPLOYER: _____

SPOUSE'S WORK TELEPHONE: _____

SPOUSE'S WORK E-MAIL ADDRESS: _____

_____

DATE UPDATED: _____

ADDRESS OF SPOUSE'S EMPLOYER: _____

_____

_____

NAME & TELEPHONE OF SPOUSE'S SUPERVISOR: _____

_____

SPOUSE'S MARITAL HISTORY

NAME OF FORMER SPOUSE: _____

DATE & PLACE OF PREVIOUS MARRIAGE: _____

_____

DATE & PLACE OF DIVORCE: _____

_____

HOME ADDRESS OF FORMER SPOUSE: _____

_____

_____

HOME TELEPHONE OF FORMER SPOUSE: _____

WORK TELEPHONE OF FORMER SPOUSE: _____

_____

E-MAIL ADDRESS OF FORMER SPOUSE: _____

_____

DATE UPDATED: _____

NAME OF FORMER SPOUSE: _____

DATE & PLACE OF PREVIOUS MARRIAGE: _____

_____

DATE & PLACE OF DIVORCE: _____

_____

HOME ADDRESS OF FORMER SPOUSE: _____

_____

_____

HOME TELEPHONE OF FORMER SPOUSE: _____

WORK TELEPHONE OF FORMER SPOUSE: _____

_____

E-MAIL ADDRESS OF FORMER SPOUSE: _____

_____

DATE UPDATED: _____

SPOUSE'S CHILDREN WITH ME

NAME: _____

DATE OF BIRTH: _____

PLACE OF BIRTH: _____

SOCIAL SECURITY NUMBER: _____

ADDRESS: _____

_____

_____

TELEPHONE: _____

E-MAIL: _____

_____

NAME: _____

DATE OF BIRTH: _____

PLACE OF BIRTH: _____

SOCIAL SECURITY NUMBER: _____

ADDRESS: _____

_____

_____

TELEPHONE: _____

E-MAIL: _____

_____

DATE UPDATED: _____

SPOUSE'S CHILDREN BY PREVIOUS MARRIAGE

NAME: _____

DATE OF BIRTH: _____

PLACE OF BIRTH: _____

SOCIAL SECURITY NUMBER: _____

ADDRESS: _____

_____

_____

TELEPHONE: _____

E-MAIL: _____

_____

NAME: _____

DATE OF BIRTH: _____

PLACE OF BIRTH: _____

SOCIAL SECURITY NUMBER: _____

ADDRESS: _____

_____

_____

TELEPHONE: _____

E-MAIL: _____

_____

DATE UPDATED: _____

SPOUSE'S PARENTS

FATHER'S NAME: _____

DATE OF BIRTH: _____

PLACE OF BIRTH: _____

DATE OF DEATH(if deceased): _____

PLACE OF BURIAL: _____

CAUSE OF DEATH: _____

SOCIAL SECURITY NUMBER: _____

ADDRESS: _____

_____

_____

HOME TELEPHONE: _____

WORK TELEPHONE: _____

_____

CELLULAR TELEPHONE: _____

E-MAIL: _____

_____

MOTHER'S NAME: _____

MOTHER'S MAIDEN NAME: _____

DATE OF BIRTH: _____

PLACE OF BIRTH: _____

DATE OF DEATH(if deceased): _____

PLACE OF BURIAL: _____

DATE UPDATED: _____

CAUSE OF DEATH: _____

SOCIAL SECURITY NUMBER: _____

ADDRESS: _____

_____

_____

HOME TELEPHONE: _____

WORK TELEPHONE: _____

_____

CELLULAR TELEPHONE: _____

E-MAIL: _____

_____

SPOUSE'S SIBLINGS

NAME: _____

DATE OF BIRTH: _____

PLACE OF BIRTH: _____

SOCIAL SECURITY NUMBER: _____

ADDRESS: _____

_____

_____

HOME TELEPHONE: _____

WORK TELEPHONE: _____

_____

DATE UPDATED: _____

CELLULAR TELEPHONE: _____

E-MAIL: _____

_____

NAME: _____

DATE OF BIRTH: _____

PLACE OF BIRTH: _____

SOCIAL SECURITY NUMBER: _____

ADDRESS: _____

_____

_____

HOME TELEPHONE: _____

WORK TELEPHONE: _____

_____

CELLULAR TELEPHONE: _____

E-MAIL: _____

_____

DATE UPDATED: _____

SPOUSE'S GRANDCHILDREN

NAME: _____

DATE OF BIRTH: _____

PLACE OF BIRTH: _____

SOCIAL SECURITY NUMBER: _____

ADDRESS: _____

_____

_____

TELEPHONE: _____

E-MAIL: _____

_____

NAME: _____

DATE OF BIRTH: _____

PLACE OF BIRTH: _____

SOCIAL SECURITY NUMBER: _____

ADDRESS: _____

_____

_____

TELEPHONE: _____

E-MAIL: _____

_____

DATE UPDATED: _____

MY FAMILY HISTORY

PARENTS

FATHER'S NAME: _____

DATE OF BIRTH: _____

PLACE OF BIRTH: _____

DATE OF DEATH(if deceased): _____

PLACE OF BURIAL: _____

CAUSE OF DEATH: _____

SOCIAL SECURITY NUMBER: _____

ADDRESS: _____

_____

_____

HOME TELEPHONE: _____

WORK TELEPHONE: _____

_____

CELLULAR TELEPHONE: _____

E-MAIL: _____

_____

MOTHER'S NAME: _____

MOTHER'S MAIDEN NAME: _____

DATE OF BIRTH: _____

DATE UPDATED: _____

PLACE OF BIRTH: _____

DATE OF DEATH(if deceased): _____

PLACE OF BURIAL: _____

CAUSE OF DEATH: _____

SOCIAL SECURITY NUMBER: _____

ADDRESS: _____

_____

_____

HOME TELEPHONE: _____

WORK TELEPHONE: _____

_____

CELLULAR TELEPHONE: _____

E-MAIL: _____

_____

SIBLINGS

NAME: _____

DATE OF BIRTH: _____

PLACE OF BIRTH: _____

SOCIAL SECURITY NUMBER: _____

ADDRESS: _____

_____

_____

DATE UPDATED: _____

HOME TELEPHONE: _____

WORK TELEPHONE: _____

_____

CELLULAR TELEPHONE: _____

E-MAIL: _____

_____

NAME: _____

DATE OF BIRTH: _____

PLACE OF BIRTH: _____

SOCIAL SECURITY NUMBER: _____

ADDRESS: _____

_____

_____

HOME TELEPHONE: _____

WORK TELEPHONE: _____

_____

CELLULAR TELEPHONE: _____

E-MAIL: _____

_____

DATE UPDATED: _____

MY CHILDREN

NAME: _____

DATE OF BIRTH: _____

PLACE OF BIRTH: _____

SOCIAL SECURITY NUMBER: _____

CURRENT ADDRESS: _____

_____

_____

CURRENT TELEPHONE: _____

E-MAIL: _____

_____

NAME: _____

DATE OF BIRTH: _____

PLACE OF BIRTH: _____

SOCIAL SECURITY NUMBER: _____

CURRENT ADDRESS: _____

_____

_____

CURRENT TELEPHONE: _____

E-MAIL: _____

_____

DATE UPDATED: _____

GRANDCHILDREN

NAME: _____

DATE OF BIRTH: _____

PLACE OF BIRTH: _____

SOCIAL SECURITY NUMBER: _____

ADDRESS: _____

_____

_____

TELEPHONE: _____

E-MAIL: _____

_____

NAME: _____

DATE OF BIRTH: _____

PLACE OF BIRTH: _____

SOCIAL SECURITY NUMBER: _____

ADDRESS: _____

_____

_____

TELEPHONE: _____

E-MAIL: _____

_____

DATE UPDATED: _____

MEDICAL INFORMATION

BLOOD TYPE

MY BLOOD TYPE: _____

MY SPOUSE'S BLOOD TYPE _____

MY CHILDREN'S BLOOD TYPES _____

_____

MEDICATIONS
(Include eyeglasses, if applicable.)

MY MEDICATIONS

    NAME OF MEDICINE: _____

    DOCTOR PRESCRIBING: _____

    PRESCRIPTION NUMBER: _____

    DOSAGE: _____

    NAME OF MEDICINE: _____

    DOCTOR PRESCRIBING: _____

    PRESCRIPTION NUMBER: _____

    DOSAGE: _____

    NAME OF MEDICINE: _____

    DOCTOR PRESCRIBING: _____

    PRESCRIPTION NUMBER: _____

    DOSAGE: _____

DATE UPDATED: _____

NAME OF MEDICINE: _____

DOCTOR PRESCRIBING: _____

PRESCRIPTION NUMBER: _____

DOSAGE: _____

MY SPOUSE'S MEDICATIONS

NAME OF MEDICINE: _____

DOCTOR PRESCRIBING: _____

PRESCRIPTION NUMBER: _____

DOSAGE: _____

NAME OF MEDICINE: _____

DOCTOR PRESCRIBING: _____

PRESCRIPTION NUMBER: _____

DOSAGE: _____

NAME OF MEDICINE: _____

DOCTOR PRESCRIBING: _____

PRESCRIPTION NUMBER: _____

DOSAGE: _____

DATE UPDATED: _____

NAME OF MEDICINE: _____

DOCTOR PRESCRIBING: _____

PRESCRIPTION NUMBER: _____

DOSAGE: _____

MY CHILDREN'S MEDICATIONS

NAME OF MEDICINE: _____

DOCTOR PRESCRIBING: _____

PRESCRIPTION NUMBER: _____

DOSAGE: _____

NAME OF MEDICINE: _____

DOCTOR PRESCRIBING: _____

PRESCRIPTION NUMBER: _____

DOSAGE: _____

NAME OF MEDICINE: _____

DOCTOR PRESCRIBING: _____

PRESCRIPTION NUMBER: _____

DOSAGE: _____

DATE UPDATED: _____

NAME OF MEDICINE: _____

DOCTOR PRESCRIBING: _____

PRESCRIPTION NUMBER: _____

DOSAGE: _____

ALLERGIES

MY ALLERGIES _____

_____

MY SPOUSE'S ALLERGIES _____

_____

MY CHILDREN'S ALLERGIES _____

_____

_____

_____

VACCINATION RECORDS

LOCATION OF MY RECORDS: _____

_____

LOCATION OF MY SPOUSE'S RECORDS: _____

_____

LOCATION OF CHILDREN'S RECORDS: _____

_____

DATE UPDATED: _____

HOSPITAL

HOSPITAL NEAREST MY HOME (include name & address): _____

_____

_____

TELEPHONE: _____

HOSPITAL I PREFER (include name & address): _____

_____

_____

TELEPHONE: _____

MISCELLANEOUS

MEDICARE NUMBERS: _____

_____

MEDICAID NUMBERS: _____

_____

    CASEWORKER NUMBERS, ADDRESS/TELEPHONE): _____

_____

_____

SOCIAL WORKER OR CASEWORKER NAMES & CONTACT INFO: _____

_____

_____

DATE UPDATED: _____

GENERAL PRACTITIONER

NAME: _____

ADDRESS: _____

_____

_____

TELEPHONE: _____

E-MAIL: _____

_____

DENTIST

NAME: _____

ADDRESS: _____

_____

_____

TELEPHONE: _____

E-MAIL: _____

_____

DATE UPDATED: _____

OTHER DOCTORS

NAME: _____

TYPE OF DOCTOR: _____

ADDRESS: _____

_____

_____

TELEPHONE: _____

E-MAIL: _____

_____

NAME: _____

TYPE OF DOCTOR: _____

ADDRESS: _____

_____

_____

TELEPHONE: _____

E-MAIL: _____

_____

DATE UPDATED: _____

NAME: _____

TYPE OF DOCTOR: _____

ADDRESS: _____

_____

_____

TELEPHONE: _____

E-MAIL: _____

_____

NAME: _____

TYPE OF DOCTOR: _____

ADDRESS: _____

_____

_____

TELEPHONE: _____

E-MAIL: _____

_____

DATE UPDATED: _____

NAME: _____

TYPE OF DOCTOR: _____

ADDRESS: _____

_____

_____

TELEPHONE: _____

E-MAIL: _____

_____

NAME: _____

TYPE OF DOCTOR: _____

ADDRESS: _____

_____

_____

TELEPHONE: _____

E-MAIL: _____

_____

DATE UPDATED: _____

TO NOTIFY IN CASE OF EMERGENCY
(Include family and business contacts)

NAME: _____

HOME TELEPHONE: _____

WORK TELEPHONE: _____

_____

CELLULAR TELEPHONE: _____

RELATIONSHIP: _____

ADDRESS: _____

_____

_____

E-MAIL: _____

_____

NAME: _____

HOME TELEPHONE: _____

WORK TELEPHONE: _____

_____

CELLULAR TELEPHONE: _____

RELATIONSHIP: _____

ADDRESS: _____

_____

_____

E-MAIL: _____

_____

DATE UPDATED: _____

NAME: _____

HOME TELEPHONE: _____

WORK TELEPHONE: _____

_____

CELLULAR TELEPHONE: _____

RELATIONSHIP: _____

ADDRESS: _____

_____

_____

E-MAIL: _____

_____

NAME: _____

HOME TELEPHONE: _____

WORK TELEPHONE: _____

_____

CELLULAR TELEPHONE: _____

RELATIONSHIP: _____

ADDRESS: _____

_____

_____

E-MAIL: _____

_____

DATE UPDATED: _____

MY LEGAL DOCUMENTS

SOCIAL SECURITY

NUMBER: _____

LOCATION OF CARD: _____

_____

PASSPORT & NATURALIZATION PAPERS

MY PASSPORT NUMBER: _____

PASSPORT NUMBERS OF FAMILY MEMBERS:

    NAME: _____

    NUMBER: _____

    LOCATION: _____

    NAME: _____

    NUMBER: _____

    LOCATION: _____

    NAME: _____

    NUMBER: _____

    LOCATION: _____

DATE UPDATED: _____

NAME: _____

NUMBER: _____

LOCATION: _____

NAME: _____

NUMBER: _____

LOCATION: _____

DATE OF MY NATURALIZATION: _____

LOCATION OF MY NATURALIZATION PAPERS: _____
_____

NATURALIZATION OF FAMILY MEMBERS:

NAME: _____

DATE: _____

LOCATION: _____

NAME: _____

DATE: _____

LOCATION: _____

NAME: _____

DATE: _____

LOCATION: _____

DATE UPDATED: _____

NAME: _____

DATE: _____

LOCATION: _____

NAME: _____

DATE: _____

LOCATION: _____

BIRTH & ADOPTION CERTIFICATES

LOCATION OF MY BIRTH CERTIFICATE: _____
_____

LOCATION OF SPOUSE'S & CHILDRENS' CERTIFICATES: _____
_____

DATE UPDATED: _____

WILL

DATE: _____

LOCATION: _____

_____

EXECUTOR: _____

ATTORNEY: _____

    LAW FIRM: _____

    ADDRESS: _____

    _____

    _____

    TELEPHONE: _____

    E-MAIL: _____

OTHER DOCUMENTS (living will, advance directive, "Five Wishes," DNR, etc.)

LOCATION OF DOCUMENTS: _____

MY "HEALTH CARE AGENTS"
    FIRST CHOICE NAME: _____

    ADDRESS: _____

    _____

    _____

    TELEPHONE: _____

    E-MAIL: _____

DATE UPDATED: _____

SECOND CHOICE NAME: _____

ADDRESS: _____

_____

_____

TELEPHONE: _____

E-MAIL: _____

POWER OF ATTORNEY

WHO HAS MY POWER OF ATTORNEY?

_____

_____

LOCATION OF (ORIGINAL) POWER OF ATTORNEY DOCUMENTS: _____

_____

WHO HAS MY POWER OF ATTORNEY (in case of change)?

_____

_____

LOCATION OF (ORIGINAL) POWER OF ATTORNEY DOCUMENTS: _____

_____

DATE UPDATED: _____

LEGAL GUARDIANSHIP

NAME OF PERSON FOR WHOM I HAVE LEGAL GUARDIANSHIP: _____

_____

LOCATION OF DOCUMENT: _____

_____

ATTORNEY: _____

   LAW FIRM: _____

   ADDRESS: _____

   _____

   _____

   TELEPHONE: _____

   E-MAIL: _____

TRUST FUNDS

TYPE: _____

BENEFICIARY: _____

ATTORNEY: _____

   LAW FIRM: _____

   ADDRESS: _____

   _____

   _____

   TELEPHONE: _____

   E- MAIL: _____

TYPE: _____

BENEFICIARY: _____

ATTORNEY: _____

    LAW FIRM: _____

    ADDRESS: _____

    _____

    _____

    TELEPHONE: _____

    E-MAIL: _____

INHERITANCE

DETAILS REGARDING INHERITANCES DUE TO ME: _____

_____

_____

_____

_____

_____

_____

_____

LOCATION OF RELEVANT DOCUMENTS: _____

_____

DATE UPDATED: _____

LEASE

NAME OF LESSOR: _____

ADDRESS: _____

_____

_____

TELEPHONE: _____

E-MAIL: _____

ADDRESS OF RENTED PROPERTY: _____

_____

_____

TYPE OF PROPERTY (apartment, vacation cottage, house, stable, etc.): _____

_____

RENT (include amount & due date): _____

_____

EXPIRATION DATE: _____

LOCATION OF LEASE DOCUMENT: _____

_____

NAME OF LESSOR: _____

ADDRESS: _____

_____

_____

TELEPHONE: _____

DATE UPDATED: _____

E-MAIL: _____

ADDRESS OF RENTED PROPERTY: _____

_____

_____

TYPE OF PROPERTY (apartment, vacation cottage, house, stable, etc.): _____

_____

RENT (include amount & due date): _____

_____

EXPIRATION DATE: _____

LOCATION OF LEASE DOCUMENT: _____

_____

NAME OF LESSOR: _____

ADDRESS: _____

_____

_____

TELEPHONE: _____

E-MAIL: _____

ADDRESS OF RENTED PROPERTY: _____

_____

_____

TYPE OF PROPERTY (apartment, vacation cottage, house, stable, etc.): _____

_____

DATE UPDATED: _____

RENT (include amount & due date): _____

_____

EXPIRATION DATE: _____

LOCATION OF LEASE DOCUMENT: _____

_____

HOUSEHOLD EFFECTS INVENTORY

LOCATION OF INVENTORY LIST (including list of jewelry & valuables): _____

_____

ITEMS IN STORAGE (include inventory; storage bin number; name & address of storage company & amount of monthly payment; & any insurance coverage)

_____

_____

_____

_____

_____

_____

_____

_____

_____

_____

DATE UPDATED: _____

MY INSURANCE POLICIES

HEALTH INSURANCE

COMPANY: _____

ADDRESS: _____

_____

_____

FEDERAL PLAN? _____

MEMBER NUMBER: _____

GROUP POLICY NUMBER: _____

PERSONS COVERED: _____

_____

_____

ADDITIONAL COVERAGE: _____

PAYMENT (include amount & due date, if not deducted automatically from salary): _____

_____

LOCATION OF POLICY: _____

MEDICARE NUMBERS: _____

_____

MEDICAID NUMBERS: _____

_____

(CASEWORKER NUMBERS, ADDRESS/TELEPHONE): _____

_____

_____

DATE UPDATED: _____

LONG TERM CARE INSURANCE

COMPANY: _____

ADDRESS: _____

_____

_____

POLICY NUMBER: _____

PAYMENT (include amount & due date): _____

LOCATION OF POLICY: _____

LIFE INSURANCE

COMPANY: _____

AMOUNT: _____

BENEFICIARY: _____

_____

LOCATION OF POLICY: _____

SPOUSE'S LIFE INSURANCE POLICY & COMPANY: _____

_____

POLICIES ON SPOUSE & CHILDREN: _____

_____

PAYMENT (include amount & due date): _____

LOCATION OF POLICY: _____

DATE UPDATED: _____

DISABILITY INSURANCE

NAME: _____

ADDRESS: _____

_____

_____

MEMBER NUMBER: _____

LOCATION OF POLICY: _____

PROFESSIONAL INSURANCE

COMPANY: _____

ADDRESS: _____

_____

_____

MEMBER NUMBER: _____

GROUP POLICY NUMBER: _____

PAYMENT (include amount & due date): _____

LOCATION OF POLICY: _____

DATE UPDATED: _____

PROPERTY INSURANCE

MORTGAGE INSURANCE COMPANY: _____

_____

POLICY NUMBER: _____

ADDRESS: _____

_____

_____

PAYMENT (include amount & due date): _____

LOCATION OF MORTGAGE INSURANCE POLICY: _____

_____

HOMEOWNER'S INSURANCE COMPANY: _____

_____

POLICY NUMBER: _____

ADDRESS: _____

_____

_____

PAYMENT (include amount & due date): _____

LOCATION OF HOMEOWNER'S INSURANCE POLICY: _____

_____

DATE UPDATED: _____

MORTGAGE INSURANCE COMPANY: _____

_____

POLICY NUMBER: _____

ADDRESS: _____

_____

_____

PAYMENT (include amount & due date): _____

LOCATION OF MORTGAGE INSURANCE POLICY: _____

_____

HOMEOWNER'S INSURANCE COMPANY: _____

_____

POLICY NUMBER: _____

ADDRESS: _____

_____

_____

PAYMENT (include amount & due date): _____

LOCATION OF HOMEOWNER'S INSURANCE POLICY: _____

_____

DATE UPDATED: _____

VEHICLE INSURANCE

COMPANY: _____

ADDRESS: _____

_____

_____

POLICY NUMBER: _____

PAYMENT (include amount & due date): _____

LOCATION OF POLICY: _____

COMPANY: _____

ADDRESS: _____

_____

_____

POLICY NUMBER: _____

PAYMENT (include amount & due date): _____

LOCATION OF POLICY: _____

COMPANY: _____

ADDRESS: _____

POLICY NUMBER: _____

PAYMENT (include amount & due date): _____

LOCATION OF POLICY: _____

DATE UPDATED: _____

COMPANY: _____

ADDRESS: _____

_____

_____

POLICY NUMBER: _____

PAYMENT (include amount & due date): _____

LOCATION OF POLICY: _____

COMPANY: _____

ADDRESS: _____

_____

_____

POLICY NUMBER: _____

PAYMENT (include amount & due date): _____

LOCATION OF POLICY: _____

DATE UPDATED: _____

MY EMPLOYMENT

CURRENT EMPLOYER / BUSINESS

NAME OF EMPLOYER: _____

NAME OF OFFICE: _____

ADDRESS: _____

_____

_____

MY WORK TELEPHONE: _____

_____

MY WORK E-MAIL ADDRESS: _____

DATES OF MY EMPLOYMENT: _____

MY CURRENT TITLE: _____

MY CURRENT RANK: _____

NAME OF SUPERVISOR: _____

TELEPHONE OF SUPERVISOR: _____

E-MAIL OF SUPERVISOR: _____

BUSINESS LICENSE INFORMATION: _____

_____

DATE UPDATED: _____

NAME OF EMPLOYER: _____

NAME OF OFFICE: _____

ADDRESS: _____

_____

_____

MY WORK TELEPHONE: _____

_____

MY WORK E-MAIL ADDRESS: _____

DATES OF MY EMPLOYMENT: _____

MY CURRENT TITLE: _____

MY CURRENT RANK: _____

NAME OF SUPERVISOR: _____

TELEPHONE OF SUPERVISOR: _____

E-MAIL OF SUPERVISOR: _____

BUSINESS LICENSE INFORMATION: _____

_____

DATE UPDATED: _____

SALARY

ANNUAL SALARY: _____

FREQUENCY OF PAYMENT: _____

AUTOMATIC DEDUCTIONS (include account & amount): _____

_____

_____

LOCATION OF EARNINGS & LEAVE STATEMENTS: _____

_____

LEAVE PROGRAM

ANNUAL LEAVE BALANCE: _____

SICK LEAVE BALANCE: _____

HOME LEAVE BALANCE: _____

MEMBER OF A MEDICAL LEAVE SHARING PLAN? _____

    BENEFICIARY: _____

_____

DATE UPDATED: _____

PREVIOUS EMPLOYMENT

LOCATION OF RECORDS OF PREVIOUS EMPLOYMENT: _____

_____

_____

RETIREMENT

RETIREMENT SYSTEM: _____

_____

DATE OF ELIGIBILITY FOR RETIREMENT: _____

_____

DUE TO PRIOR MILITARY SERVICE OR FEDERAL SERVICE, I HAVE BEEN ADVISED THAT I MAY NEED TO PAY EITHER A DEPOSIT OR A RE-DEPOSIT TO FULLY RECEIVE CREDIT FOR THAT SERVICE: YES   NO

HAVE DEPOSITS/RE-DEPOSITS BEEN PAID?   YES   NO

IF MY DEATH OCCURS BEFORE RETIREMENT, MY SPOUSE IS AWARE THAT S/HE MAY BE ELIGIBLE FOR A SURVIVOR ANNUITY?
     YES   NO

AMOUNT PER MONTH: _____

RESTRICTIONS/LIMITATIONS: _____

_____

IF I AM A FEDERAL EMPLOYEE UNDER FERS, IS MY SPOUSE AWARE S/HE & THE CHILDREN MAY QUALIFY FOR SOCIAL SECURITY BENEFITS?
     YES   NO

DATE UPDATED: _____

MY MILITARY SERVICE

MILITARY ID NUMBER: _____

BRANCH OF SERVICE: _____

YEARS OF SERVICE: _____

RANK AT SEPARATION: _____

LOCATION OF RECORD OF MILITARY SERVICE (DD 214): _____

_____

DATE UPDATED: _____

MY FINANCIAL INFORMATION

BANK ACCOUNTS

BANK: _____

ADDRESS: _____

_____

_____

CHECKING ACCOUNT NUMBER: _____

    IS THIS A JOINT ACCOUNT? WITH WHOM? _____

    _____

    IS THERE A DEBTOR CARD(S) ISSUED ON THIS ACCOUNT? _____

    _____

SAVINGS ACCOUNT NUMBER: _____

    IS THIS A JOINT ACCOUNT? WITH WHOM? _____

    _____

ATM CARD NUMBER & PIN NUMBER: _____

_____

LOCATION OF CHECKBOOKS, STATEMENTS, & OTHER INFO: _____

_____

DATE UPDATED: _____

BANK: _____

ADDRESS: _____

_____

_____

CHECKING ACCOUNT NUMBER: _____

    IS THIS A JOINT ACCOUNT? WITH WHOM? _____

_____

    IS THERE A DEBTOR CARD(S) ISSUED ON THIS ACCOUNT? _____

_____

SAVINGS ACCOUNT NUMBER: _____

    IS THIS A JOINT ACCOUNT? WITH WHOM? _____

_____

ATM CARD NUMBER & PIN NUMBER: _____

_____

LOCATION OF CHECKBOOKS, STATEMENTS, & OTHER INFO: _____

_____

DATE UPDATED: _____

INVESTMENTS:
(Include IRAs, TSP/401Ks, Certificates of Deposit, Stocks, Bonds, etc.)

ACCOUNT NUMBER: _____

TYPE: _____

COMPANY: _____

BENEFICIARY: _____

LOCATION OF RECORDS: _____

_____

ACCOUNT NUMBER: _____

TYPE: _____

COMPANY: _____

BENEFICIARY: _____

LOCATION OF RECORDS: _____

_____

ACCOUNT NUMBER: _____

TYPE: _____

COMPANY: _____

BENEFICIARY: _____

LOCATION OF RECORDS: _____

_____

DATE UPDATED: _____

SAFETY DEPOSIT BOX

SAFETY DEPOSIT BOX NUMBER: _____

BANK: _____

ADDRESS: _____

_____

_____

ACCESSIBLE BY: _____

LOCATION OF KEY: _____

CONTENTS: _____

_____

_____

_____

_____

_____

DATE UPDATED: _____

CREDIT CARDS

NAME: _____

ACCOUNT NUMBER: _____

PIN NUMBER: _____

ISSUED BY: _____

ADDRESS: _____

_____

_____

IS ACCOUNT BALANCE INSURED? _____

_____

LOCATION OF STATEMENTS & OTHER INFO: _____

_____

NAME: _____

ACCOUNT NUMBER: _____

PIN NUMBER: _____

ISSUED BY: _____

ADDRESS: _____

_____

_____

IS ACCOUNT BALANCE INSURED? _____

_____

LOCATION OF STATEMENTS & OTHER INFO: _____

_____

DATE UPDATED: _____

FINANCIAL ADVISOR / PLANNER / MANAGER / ACCOUNTANT

NAME & TITLE: _____

NAME OF BUSINESS: _____

ADDRESS: _____

_____

_____

TELEPHONE: _____

E-MAIL: _____

NAME & TITLE: _____

NAME OF BUSINESS: _____

ADDRESS: _____

_____

_____

TELEPHONE: _____

E-MAIL: _____

NAME & TITLE: _____

NAME OF BUSINESS: _____

ADDRESS: _____

_____

_____

TELEPHONE: _____

E-MAIL: _____

DATE UPDATED: _____

RECORDS OF OTHER DEBTS OWED BY ME

DEBT OWED TO: _____

ADDRESS: _____

_____

_____

TELEPHONE: _____

TYPE OF DEBT: _____

AMOUNT: _____

DUE DATE: _____

LOCATION OF DOCUMENTATION: _____

_____

DEBT OWED TO: _____

ADDRESS: _____

_____

_____

TELEPHONE: _____

TYPE OF DEBT: _____

AMOUNT: _____

DUE DATE: _____

LOCATION OF DOCUMENTATION: _____

_____

DATE UPDATED: _____

RECORDS OF ANY DEBT OWED TO ME

NAME OF DEBTOR: _____

ADDRESS: _____

_____

_____

TELEPHONE: _____

TYPE OF DEBT: _____

AMOUNT: _____

DUE DATE: _____

LOCATION OF DOCUMENTATION: _____

_____

NAME OF DEBTOR: _____

ADDRESS: _____

_____

_____

TELEPHONE: _____

TYPE OF DEBT: _____

AMOUNT: _____

DUE DATE: _____

LOCATION OF DOCUMENTATION: _____

_____

DATE UPDATED: _____

INCOME TAXES

LOCATION OF TAX RETURNS/RECORDS: _____
_____

NAME & ADDRESS OF TAX PREPARER: _____
_____
_____

FINANCIAL INFORMATION OF SPOUSE & CHILDREN

_____
_____
_____
_____
_____
_____
_____
_____
_____
_____
_____
_____

DATE UPDATED: _____

MY REAL ESTATE

TYPE OF PROPERTY (stand alone house? apartment? townhouse? warehouse? office building? other?): _____

JOINT OWNERSHIP? _____

ADDRESS: _____

_____

_____

LOCATION OF DEED: _____

VALUE OF PROPERTY: _____

PROPERTY MANAGEMENT COMPANY: _____

_____

MORTGAGE ON THE PROPERTY IS HELD BY: _____

ADDRESS: _____

_____

_____

BALANCE OF LOAN: _____

MONTHLY PAYMENT (amount & due date): _____

LOCATION OF MORTGAGE & TAX PAYMENT DOCUMENTS & RECEIPTS: _____

_____

MORTGAGE INSURANCE: _____

LOCATION OF MORTGAGE INSURANCE POLICY: _____

_____

HOMEOWNER'S INSURANCE HELD BY: _____

LOCATION OF HOMEOWNER'S INSURANCE POLICY: _____

_____

DATE UPDATED: _____

TYPE OF PROPERTY (stand alone house? apartment? townhouse? warehouse? office building? other?): _____

JOINT OWNERSHIP? _____

ADDRESS: _____

_____

_____

LOCATION OF DEED: _____

VALUE OF PROPERTY: _____

PROPERTY MANAGEMENT COMPANY: _____

_____

MORTGAGE ON THE PROPERTY IS HELD BY: _____

ADDRESS: _____

_____

_____

BALANCE OF LOAN: _____

MONTHLY PAYMENT (amount & due date): _____

LOCATION OF MORTGAGE & TAX PAYMENT DOCUMENTS & RECEIPTS: _____

_____

MORTGAGE INSURANCE: _____

LOCATION OF MORTGAGE INSURANCE POLICY: _____

_____

HOMEOWNER'S INSURANCE HELD BY: _____

LOCATION OF HOMEOWNER'S INSURANCE POLICY: _____

_____

DATE UPDATED: _____

UTILITIES

ADDRESS WHERE PAID:

ELECTRICITY

COMPANY: _____

ACCOUNT NUMBER: _____

WATER

COMPANY: _____

ACCOUNT NUMBER: _____

GAS

COMPANY: _____

ACCOUNT NUMBER: _____

TELEPHONES

COMPANY: _____

ACCOUNT NUMBER: _____

TELEPHONE NUMBER: _____

COMPANY: _____

ACCOUNT NUMBER: _____

TELEPHONE NUMBER: _____

DATE UPDATED: _____

NEWSPAPER

COMPANY: _____

ACCOUNT NUMBER: _____

INTERNET SERVICE

COMPANY: _____

ACCOUNT NUMBER: _____

LOGON NAME: _____

PASSWORD: _____

CABLE TELEVISION

COMPANY: _____

ACCOUNT NUMBER: _____

LOGON NAME: _____

PASSWORD: _____

DATE UPDATED: _____

OTHER SUBSCRIPTIONS

COMPANY: _____

ACCOUNT NUMBER: _____

LOGON NAME: _____

PASSWORD: _____

COMPANY: _____

ACCOUNT NUMBER: _____

LOGON NAME: _____

PASSWORD: _____

COMPANY: _____

ACCOUNT NUMBER: _____

LOGON NAME: _____

PASSWORD: _____

COMPANY: _____

ACCOUNT NUMBER: _____

LOGON NAME: _____

PASSWORD: _____

DATE UPDATED: _____

MY VEHICLES

TYPE (sedan? SUV? truck? minivan? other?): _____

MAKE: _____

MODEL: _____

YEAR: _____

REGISTERED TO (include location of registration document): _____
_____

STATUS OF OWNERSHIP (lien? own? lease?): _____

    BANK/CREDITOR THAT HANDLES LOAN: _____
_____

    ADDRESS: _____
_____
_____

    PAYMENT (amount & due date): _____

    BALANCE: _____

    LOCATION OF LOAN PAPERS & INVOICES: _____
_____

VIN NUMBER: _____

LICENSE PLATE NUMBER: _____

LOCATION OF TITLE: _____

LOCATION OF EXTRA KEYS: _____

INSURED BY: _____

                                  DATE UPDATED: _____

ADDRESS OF INSURANCE COMPANY: _____

_____

_____

INSURANCE POLICY NUMBER: _____

LOCATION OF INSURANCE POLICY: _____

_____

TYPE (sedan? SUV? truck? minivan? other?): _____

MAKE: _____

MODEL: _____

YEAR: _____

REGISTERED TO (include location of registration document): _____

_____

STATUS OF OWNERSHIP (lien? own? lease?): _____

    BANK/CREDITOR THAT HANDLES LOAN: _____

    _____

    ADDRESS: _____

    _____

    _____

    PAYMENT (amount & due date): _____

    BALANCE: _____

    LOCATION OF LOAN PAPERS & INVOICES: _____

    _____

DATE UPDATED: _____

VIN NUMBER: _____

LICENSE PLATE NUMBER: _____

LOCATION OF TITLE: _____

LOCATION OF EXTRA KEYS: _____

INSURED BY: _____

ADDRESS OF INSURANCE COMPANY: _____

_____

_____

INSURANCE POLICY NUMBER: _____

LOCATION OF INSURANCE POLICY: _____

_____

DATE UPDATED: _____

MY PETS

NAME: _____

TYPE: _____

BREED: _____

SEX: MALE   FEMALE

NEUTERED?   YES   NO

DATE OF BIRTH: _____

MEDICAL PROBLEMS: _____

_____

DIET: _____

SPECIAL NEEDS: _____

_____

LOCATION OF RECORDS (vaccination, AKC registration, etc.): _____

_____

DISPOSITION IN CASE OF MY DEATH: _____

_____

NAME: _____

TYPE: _____

BREED: _____

SEX: MALE   FEMALE

NEUTERED?   YES   NO

DATE OF BIRTH: _____

DATE UPDATED: _____

MEDICAL PROBLEMS: _____
_____

DIET: _____

SPECIAL NEEDS: _____
_____

LOCATION OF RECORDS (vaccination, AKC registration, etc.): _____
_____

DISPOSITION IN CASE OF MY DEATH: _____

NAME: _____

TYPE: _____

BREED: _____

SEX: MALE   FEMALE

NEUTERED?   YES   NO

DATE OF BIRTH: _____

MEDICAL PROBLEMS: _____
_____

DIET: _____

SPECIAL NEEDS: _____
_____

LOCATION OF RECORDS (vaccination, AKC registration, etc.): _____
_____

DISPOSITION IN CASE OF MY DEATH: _____

DATE UPDATED: _____

VETERINARIAN

NAME: _____

ADDRESS: _____

_____

_____

TELEPHONE: _____

E-MAIL: _____

PET INSURANCE

COMPANY: _____

POLICY NUMBER: _____

ADDRESS: _____

_____

_____

TELEPHONE: _____

E-MAIL: _____

DATE UPDATED: _____

MY MEMBERSHIPS & CHARITIES

(Include professional and recreational memberships)

NAME OF ORGANIZATION: _____

ADDRESS: _____

_____

_____

TELEPHONE: _____

MY MEMBERSHIP NUMBER: _____

NAME OF ORGANIZATION: _____

ADDRESS: _____

_____

_____

TELEPHONE: _____

MY MEMBERSHIP NUMBER: _____

NAME OF ORGANIZATION: _____

ADDRESS: _____

_____

_____

TELEPHONE: _____

MY MEMBERSHIP NUMBER: _____

DATE UPDATED: _____

NAME OF ORGANIZATION: _____

ADDRESS: _____

_____

_____

TELEPHONE: _____

MY MEMBERSHIP NUMBER: _____

NAME OF ORGANIZATION: _____

ADDRESS: _____

_____

_____

TELEPHONE: _____

MY MEMBERSHIP NUMBER: _____

DATE UPDATED: _____

FUNERAL ARRANGEMENTS

RELIGIOUS AFFILIATION: _____

CHURCH: _____

    ADDRESS: _____

    _____

    _____

    TELEPHONE: _____

FUNERAL SERVICES

TYPE OF SERVICE: _____

PLACE: _____

TIME: _____

CLERGY: _____

    ADDRESS: _____

    _____

    _____

    TELEPHONE: _____

    E-MAIL: _____

SPECIAL REQUESTS FOR SERVICE (music, flowers, readings, etc.): _____

_____

_____

_____

_____

DATE UPDATED: _____

AM I ENTITLED TO MILITARY HONORS?   YES   NO

WHO WOULD I LIKE TO DO THE EULOGY? _____

    ADDRESS: _____

_____

_____

    TELEPHONE: _____

    E-MAIL: _____

WHO WOULD I ESPECIALLY LIKE TO ATTEND?

_____

_____

_____

_____

OBITUARY

DO I WANT AN OBITUARY PUBLISHED? _____

WHERE? _____

WHAT I WANT INCLUDED IN THE OBITUARY: _____

_____

_____

_____

_____

DATE UPDATED: _____

DISPOSITION OF REMAINS

ORGAN DONOR?   YES   NO

    SPECIAL INSTRUCTIONS FOR ORGAN DONATION: _____

_____

_____

_____

_____

FUNERAL HOME PREFERENCE: _____

    ADDRESS: _____

_____

_____

    TELEPHONE: _____

BURIAL (casket, vault, crypt)? _____

    MY CHOICE OF CEMETARY: _____

    PRE-PAID BURIAL PLAN? _____

    LOCATION OF PLAN: _____

_____

    CLOTHING TO BE BURIED IN: _____

_____

DATE UPDATED: _____

PALLBEARERS:

NAME: _____

ADDRESS: _____

_____

_____

TELEPHONE: _____

NAME: _____

ADDRESS: _____

_____

_____

TELEPHONE: _____

NAME: _____

ADDRESS: _____

_____

_____

TELEPHONE: _____

NAME: _____

ADDRESS: _____

_____

_____

TELEPHONE: _____

DATE UPDATED: _____

CREMATION?

    WHAT I WOULD LIKE DONE WITH MY ASHES: _____

_____

_____

DONATION OF BODY?

    ORGANIZATION TO RECEIVE MY REMAINS: _____

_____

_____

_____

    ARRANGEMENTS MADE FOR THIS IN ADVANCE: _____

_____

    LOCATION OF DOCUMENTS: _____

_____

DATE UPDATED: _____

TO NOTIFY IN CASE OF DEATH
(Include family and business contacts.)

NAME: _____

HOME TELEPHONE: _____

WORK TELEPHONE: _____

RELATIONSHIP: _____

ADDRESS: _____

_____

_____

E-MAIL: _____

NAME: _____

HOME TELEPHONE: _____

WORK TELEPHONE: _____

RELATIONSHIP: _____

ADDRESS: _____

_____

_____

E-MAIL: _____

DATE UPDATED: _____

NAME: _____

HOME TELEPHONE: _____

WORK TELEPHONE: _____

RELATIONSHIP: _____

ADDRESS: _____

_____

_____

E-MAIL: _____

NAME: _____

HOME TELEPHONE: _____

WORK TELEPHONE: _____

RELATIONSHIP: _____

ADDRESS: _____

_____

_____

E-MAIL: _____

DATE UPDATED: _____

NAME: _____

HOME TELEPHONE: _____

WORK TELEPHONE: _____

RELATIONSHIP: _____

ADDRESS: _____

_____

_____

E-MAIL: _____

NAME: _____

HOME TELEPHONE: _____

WORK TELEPHONE: _____

RELATIONSHIP: _____

ADDRESS: _____

_____

_____

E-MAIL: _____

DATE UPDATED: _____

ALSO NOTIFY:
(Names & contact details listed in other sections.)

_____ EMPLOYER(S)

_____ DOCTOR(S)

_____ RELATIVES & FRIENDS IN ADDRESS BOOK & E-MAIL ADDRESS BOOK

_____ ATTORNEY

_____ ACCOUNTANT / FINANCIAL MANAGER

_____ BANK(S)

_____ BROKER(S)

_____ INSURANCE COMPANIES

_____ ORGANIZATIONS OF WHICH I AM A MEMBER

_____ OTHER _____

_____ OTHER _____

_____ OTHER _____

_____ OTHER _____

_____ OTHER _____

DATE UPDATED: _____

ADDITIONAL NOTES

ADDITIONAL NOTES

ADDITIONAL NOTES

ADDITIONAL NOTES

Made in the USA
Columbia, SC
30 November 2023